A Twisty Tale

A Twisty Tale

D.M. Culp &
L.M Simmons

Sprouting Peanut Publications

Sprouting Peanut Publications

Publisher since 2008

First Paperback Edition 2022

ISBN - 979-8-9863373-0-2

Table of Contents

If you don't like where your story is going, write a different ending.

The story you are about to read is based on Michelle's harrowing experience but delivered in a palatable way so that readers of all ages can enjoy, grow and learn from her experiences. This book is not only an account of Michelle's journey, but was, and continues to be, one of her many therapies on her road to recovery. This book was initially meant for Michelle and Michelle alone. The intention was to have her rewrite her story with a different ending than the ones offered to her by well-meaning professionals and loved ones. The consistent retelling and re-reading of Michelle's new and improved ending became ingrained in her mind, gradually shifting her expectations for all the exciting improvements that lay ahead.

Michelle insisted that her story be shared with the world.

As someone who has enjoyed participating in Michelle's recovery, it has been a pleasure to not only co-author this book with her, but to watch her new ending unfold.

Dedications

I would like to dedicate this book to all the people who help others to stand when they fall. And, of course, my husband, Chad, who makes this life that I get to live full of love, joy and a ton of laughter.

-Dawn

I would like to dedicate this book to those that have overcome challenges mentally or physically and to all the health care workers that have helped me along the path of my journey. I especially want to thank my friends and family that have helped and supported me during this challenging chapter of my life.

-Michelle

A Great, Big Name

1.

"I wonder what all the excitement is about?" squealed Pig as she watched people she had never seen before walk across the ranchette towards her pen. "New people! New people!"

Pig was a baby Chipmunk Pig that never saw much of the ranchette besides her pen. She would often spend her days alone wishing she could play with the other animals but, instead, Pig spent most days eating and sleeping alone and watching the horses run.

But not today. Today was shaping up to be an exciting day!

"Are these new people coming to see me?" Pig wondered.

A woman with long, light, silky hair and kind eyes smiled when she saw Pig. The woman didn't just smile with her lips, she smiled with her whole face. She reached down, swooped the baby pig up into her arms and asked, "Would you like to come home with me?"

Pig smiled with her whole face and nodded feverishly.

"Good. Then it's settled..." the woman said, smiling. "My name is Michelle and you're coming home with me."

Pig was delighted with this news.

"Now that you know my name, it's time to give you a name, too. What shall I call you?" Michelle thought for a moment, considering different names in her head when suddenly, it came to her!

"I know! Your name is Abigail...Abigail Claudette Von Phygg! That's spelled V-O-N P-H-Y-G-G."

Michelle declared this to be Pig's new name. She knew it was a great, big name for such a little pig so she whispered some comforting words in the little pig's ear.

"Don't worry, Abigail. Even though the spelling is fancy, it still sounds like V-O-N P-I-G."

Abigail's eyes got very wide as she knew that she would need to be a mighty pig to have such a mighty name. She nodded once again and was excited to be going to her new home with her new friend and her new name.

Exploring the Ranch

2.

Abigail had enjoyed her first car ride to her new home and was still getting used to her great, big, new name.

Now, Abigail joyfully prepared to meet all of her new friends on the farm. This was very exciting!

"Abigail, this is a very different farm than most other farms." Michelle went on to explain, "We have animals living here that don't normally live together. But don't be alarmed; all of the animals on this farm get along very nicely and everyone is very excited to meet you."

Michelle began to introduce Abigail to the animals one by one.

"Abigail, meet Mack. Mack is a Mountain Lion and she alerts the humans if there is any danger on the farm or if anyone is sick. That way, we can make sure help is on the way in case there is trouble. Mack is very good at her job. Mack, meet Abigail Claudette Von Phygg. You can call her Abby."

"Nice to meet you, Abby." Mack smiled and winked and Abby smiled back.

"Next, I'd like to introduce you to Hunter. Hunter is a Pitbull and he helps us keep order around here. Think of Hunter as our very own Farm Patrol. He protects us and makes sure we all stay safe. He is very nice but he means business. With all of these animals Hunter stays busy...but he's a good friend. Hunter, meet Abby."

"Hello, Abby." Hunter gave her a nod. "Let me know if you need anything, day or night. I sleep with one eye open." Abby nodded.

"Over here we have Princess the Rabbit. Princess works the perimeter of our farm making sure we all stay informed. Princess is really fast so she can get news to Hunter and Mack very quickly if she needs to. Princess, meet Abby." The two looked at each other and smiled.

Abby felt very comforted knowing her new friends were here to help keep the farm and everyone on it safe.

Michelle and Abby began walking across the open field when all of a sudden Abby spotted the most beautiful animal she had ever seen; so much so that she stopped and stared in awe.

"Abby, that is Princeton the Horse. He is gentle, strong and beautiful. He is my very favorite horse to ride, but shhh...don't tell the other horses."

Abby and Michelle walked to the fence line to watch Princeton run and soon Mack, Hunter and Princess all joined them. None of them said a word. They just smiled and watched Princeton gallop. Several minutes passed and not one word was spoken. All that could be heard across the farm was the rhythm of the hooves, and it sounded lovely--like music.

Michelle whispered under her breath, "I could watch him all day."

Abby agreed with a whisper, "Me, too."

Several more quiet moments passed before Michelle declared, "Ok, gang! I'm ready for dinner!"

Abby agreed with a holler, "Me, too!" But that's not surprising at all coming from a Chipmunk Pig.

A Twisty Tale

Oh, No!

3.

Days turned into weeks and weeks turned into months as Abby continued to enjoy her new home and new friends on the farm. With every passing day she became more comfortable and more at ease. It was really starting to feel like home. There were chores, routines and a whole lot of games and she was so happy to call this farm home.

The farm gave Abby many opportunities to practice different things, and she was still learning what things she did well and what she enjoyed. She figured if she could decide what she enjoyed doing, that would help her decide what her job on the farm would eventually be.

Hunter knew at a young age that he would be a protector of sorts, and Mack knew what she was going to be when she was just a cub. In fact, everyone on the farm had a job except for Abby. She didn't worry though because she was still young. She knew that one day she'd discover her true calling on this farm and that it would be crystal clear. But for now, Abby was just happy to help the grown-ups wherever she could.

One thing Abby knew for sure was that every day on the farm was a new adventure. There were still new friends she had yet to meet and areas to explore. Abby made herself a promise to introduce herself to one new friend on the farm every day.

One of Abby's favorite friends on the farm was Mae The Rooster. Abby met Mae her very first week on the farm and learned right off the bat that Mae was very protective of Michelle. That was just fine by Abby because Michelle was her favorite human. Ask any animal on the farm...if they needed to know where Michelle was or what she was doing, just ask Mae; she'd know.

Most days on the farm were fairly routine. There were feeding schedules and chores to do and repairs and maintenance were constant. There was always time for fun and games throughout the day, though. This particular day on the farm, however, was not your ordinary day. It was a day of "Oh, Nos" and not-so-fun surprises. What's more than that, it seemed like these surprises came one right after another.

The "Oh, Nos" started with Nicholas. Nicholas, the Rottweiler, was such a supportive dog - full of compassion and kindness. He had lived on the farm for nearly 8 years now and all the animals loved him. Nicholas always chose to see the good in people and didn't take to complaining. On this particular day, as he was looking to tidy up his environment, he dug a hole to store one of his bones for another time. In doing so, he accidentally broke a pipe underground. As soon as he saw the water burst from the ground, you could tell he felt awful.

Just across the farm, Whitney, one of the Zebra twins, was very excited about the daily visit from the mailman.

In all of her excitement, she accidently knocked down the front gate. No one could ever accuse Whitney of not being friendly. She'd bust down a gate if it meant getting to say hello up close.

Michelle took one look at all of the "Oh, Nos" that seemed to be happening all at once as she was filling the water trough for the horses. Mae The Rooster folded her feathers and shook her head as if to agree with Michelle that this was going to be an extra long day.

Mack the Mountain Lion made her way over to Michelle to deliver another not-so-great surprise.

"Michelle, I hate to be the bearer of more bad news, but one of the horses stepped in something awful and now he's walking funny. I think he may need some help."

"Oh, no! Which horse?" asked Michelle.

"Mr. Hyde, " said Mack.

Michelle patted Mack on the head and said, "Fine, Mack, and thanks for letting me know. Bring Mr. Hyde to the stable and tell him I'll clean his hoof as soon as I tie off the gate that Whitney busted."

Everyone had their jobs for the day. Mae decided to go oversee the situation with the broken pipe and Abby decided to head to the stall to oversee Mr. Hyde's situation while Michelle fixed the gate.

As Mack brought Mr. Hyde to the stall, Abby realized she had never met this horse before. Since Abby didn't have a job yet, she decided to help out by making polite conversation with Mr. Hyde while he waited for Michelle.

"Hello, Sir."

With a name like Mr. Hyde, she figured using a formal greeting was appropriate.

"Who are you?" Mr. Hyde sneered, seeming a bit rude, but Abby didn't let that bother her.

"My name is Abigail Claudette Von Phygg, but you can call me Abby. Do you have a first name or shall I call you Mr. Hyde?"

"Everyone on the farm teases me behind my back. They call me Jekyll, you know, like Jekyll and Hyde? They don't think I hear them make fun of me, but I do. They tease me just because I'm moody." He paused for a bit and then asked, "Do you get moody?"

Abby, not really understanding what that word meant, just shook her head.

"Of course not. You're one of those really happy pigs I bet. Well I do! I get moody. I get mad easily and sometimes I make a mess and do things I'm not supposed to just because I'm mad. And no one likes me or ever listens to me."

"That must be lonely. I'm sorry to hear that. I'll listen to you."

Abby was tender and attentive and Mr. Hyde continued to share his feelings.

"It is lonely. Very lonely," he repeated. "I don't mean to be moody; I just can't seem to help it."

Mr. Hyde seemed to be relieved to have someone to talk to. He sighed and settled down a bit.

"Thanks for listening. You are very good at it."

Abby looked around the farm and realized at this moment that she had discovered the best way she could contribute to the farm. Somehow, in the last 5 minutes, Abby found her calling. She had become a Therapy Pig and she vowed to be the best therapist this farm could ever have.

"Don't you worry, Mr. Hyde. If you ever need a friendly ear, you come and find me. I'll listen."

Abby nodded proudly as she was certain she helped Mr. Hyde take his mind off his painful hoof, if only for a moment. Indeed, Abby was shaping up to be a great therapist.

"Here comes Michelle," Abby exclaimed, "She'll fix that foot right up."

Abby backed herself into the corner allowing Michelle plenty of space to get to work. Michelle inspected the back hoof and went to her tool shed to get the proper equipment to clean the hoof. Michelle then positioned herself behind Mr. Hyde and started cleaning out his hoof as Abby stood back and watched.

Meanwhile, Mae was across the field dealing with the water gushing out of the broken pipe.

"Oh, No, Nicholas. Did you have to dig your hole here?"

Other animals joined Mae and Nicholas and started discussing different ways to fix the problem. They all agreed that they would wait until Michelle was done with Mr. Hyde before deciding what to do.

As Mae and Nicholas shared some ideas to fix the pipe, they were startled by a frightening sound. It was a squeal... a squeal so loud that all the birds on the telephone wire flew away as fast as they could. Mae looked up to see where the squeal came from and saw Abby running toward them at full speed.

"Abigail, what is it?" Mae cried.

"Oh, No!" cried Abby. "It's Michelle. She's hurt!"

Abby pointed to the stall and all of the animals looked over to see Michelle was lying on the ground. They ran over to her as quickly as they could. When they got to the stall they saw Michelle with a big bump on her head and Mr. Hyde with his head down in the corner.

"I didn't mean to hurt her. When she was cleaning my foot, something pinched. I didn't mean to kick. I didn't mean to hurt her."

Mack ran to alert the other humans on the farm to let them know there had been an accident.

Mae was right by Michelle's side.

"You're going to be alright, Michelle. Trust me, everything is going to be alright."

Abby and the others watched as Michelle was loaded into the ambulance while Hunter managed to keep the farm animals calm.

"The ambulance is going to take Michelle to the hospital and the doctors are going to take very good care of her. Michelle is in good hands," Hunter said calmly and he promised to keep all the animals informed.

Mack came over to Abby to give her some comfort because she could see that Abby was very shaken up by the accident.

"I'm so sorry you had to see that, Abby, but I'm also very glad you were there with her when it happened. You are a good friend. Do you know how excited she was the day that she went to rescue you?"

Mack's kind words helped to calm Abby. "Don't you worry. Michelle will be back. She is the strongest person I know. Just you wait and see. But you have a big job to do once she returns. She'll need you to listen to her, love her and help raise her spirits. Are you up for it?"

Abby nodded strongly with tears in her eyes. She knew, more clearly than she had known anything before, that being a Therapy Pig was her job on this farm. She also knew that she would be honored to be by Michelle's side helping to get her back on her feet.

"Yes, I'm up for it!"

Abby knew she'd be back. Somehow, she just knew it.

Nub

4.

To Abby, it seemed like an eternity since the accident. News passed around the farm that Michelle was having a difficult time recovering. Some days she seemed to get better and some days she seemed to get worse. All Abby knew was that she missed her friend dreadfully.

Princess The Rabbit was the one that came with the news today.

"I was patrolling the perimeter when I overheard some of our neighbors discussing Michelle. They said she had a rough night in the hospital last night. The doctors are saying that she'll be coming home soon but that she won't be able to talk or walk again."

All of the animals heard this news and bowed their heads in silence. While they were happy that Michelle was going to be coming home, they were sad that she wouldn't be able to talk or walk again.

Abby walked over to Princeton The Horse who seemed to take this news the hardest.

"Don't be sad, Princeton." Abby said with love in her voice. "Just because she can't ride you doesn't mean she won't come and see you. Don't tell the other horses but she told me that you were her favorite. She'll still come to visit you."

"I know," said Princeton, "It just won't be the same."

The sun set like a heavy blanket over the farm that night. No one talked about it but everyone felt it. It was sadness.

Abby found that she slept most comfortably in the horse stall these days. She made herself a cozy bed out of fresh hay and settled in for the night to look at the stars. She wondered what would happen if she made a wish on one of these stars.

"It worked for The Cricket." Abby said quietly to herself.

"Star light, star bright, first star I see tonight. I wish I may, I wish I might, have this wish I wish tonight. My wish is that my friend Michelle will be able to walk and talk again."

Abby didn't know if her wish was a prayer, an old children's poem, a wish, or a song. All she knew was it felt good to say those words out loud.

Abby closed her eyes and began to dream.

She dreamt she was asleep on a pile of hay in the stall and that she was loved and surrounded by friends. This was a nice dream. Then, out of the starry sky, a small yellow orb drifted down and landed right on the hay in front of Abby's nose. She knew it was a dream but the orb startled her just the same. The yellow orb seemed to move slowly and pulse with a gorgeous glow.

"Wow!" Said Abby. "Are you my wish that I just wished tonight?"

The glowing orb in the dream began to whisper.

"I am."

"What is your name? Do you even have a name?" Abby was wide-eyed and excited.

"You can call me Nub."

Abby was delighted. "Nub," she asked with excitement, "Did you hear the wish I made? Will my friend, Michelle, walk and talk again? Is there anything more I can do to help her?"

"Trust that Michelle is strong and brave. Trust that her mind and body know how to heal and be well. Trust that there are healing powers available to all that are far beyond your imagination. Love and support her. Remind Michelle of these things when she is tired, angry, frustrated and afraid. Share this message with all the animals on the farm. Love her and trust the process."

With that, Nub zipped off back into the night sky. Abby would always remember this as the best dream she ever had.

Homecoming

5.

Today was the day!

The farm was buzzing with all the animals preparing for Michelle's return home. Some of the animals were blowing up balloons, some of the animals were cleaning up, and some of the animals were making a sign that said, "WELCOME HOME!"

It was the first time in months that the farm felt joyful again. Michelle was coming home and everyone was excited. As the truck pulled up in the driveway, Mae was first in line to welcome Michelle home and prepare her wheelchair.

"Your chariot awaits you!" Mae said jokingly as some strong arms assisted Michelle out of the truck and into her wheelchair.

As Michelle made her way to all of the farm animals that anxiously awaited to greet her, Mae led the way like a band leader instructing folks to clear a path.

"Clear a path! Make way! We're coming through!" Mae said and she widened her wing span to direct traffic.

Michelle watched as Mae cleared a path for her arrival.

Michelle greeted each of her friends one by one, not with words, but with a smile in her eyes that seemed to say, "I see you."

Each of the animals on the farm tried to hide their sadness and managed to put on a brave face when Michelle was wheeled by them. It wasn't until Michelle was taken into the house for a nap that the animals gathered to grieve together.

"Poor Michelle," whispered Mack and Nick while all the animals fought back the tears.

It was at this moment that Abby decided to share the dream she had of Nub hoping maybe it would comfort all of them like it comforted her. Abby began to share her dream from the beginning with the golden orb and the beautiful messages. The animals were captivated, hanging on Abby's every word.

"We need to not forget that the body knows how to heal and be well. Mack, if you can heal from a cut on your paw, that same healing can take place in Michelle. We can't get discouraged, gang! We have to remember how strong she is. We have to remember how feisty she is. We have to remember how brave she is. If we forget all of those things then how can we remind her? Our job is to remind Michelle of all these things because she has forgotten! We need to love and support her and remind her that her mind and body knows how to heal and be well!"

Everyone cheered!!! All the animals were excited to pitch in and be a part of Michelle's recovery.

One of the humans came out of the house when they saw all the animals congregating in the yard.

With his head held low he announced to all the animals that Michelle would be extra tired moving forward and not to get their hopes up. The animals nodded politely and managed to keep their smiles from curling the corners of their mouths. The same thought occurred to all the animals at once.

He doesn't know about the dream.

Remembering

6.

Every morning, like clockwork, one of the humans from inside the house would wheel Michelle outside to enjoy some fresh air and sunshine. For months now all the animals on the farm took turns walking Michelle down memory lane reminding her of all the times in her life where she was brave or strong.

Today was Nicholas' turn. Nicholas sat with Michelle and recounted the story of Michelle falling out of a tree she was climbing when she was a young girl. He reminded Michelle that even though the fall hurt her legs at the time, they recovered perfectly and she was climbing trees again in no time. Michelle seemed to be extra engaged today and Nicholas was sure that as she remembered this story. She smiled at him. The smile, although it was small at first, caught everyone's attention. All the animals came running over and as the group got larger Michelle's smile got bigger. It was the prettiest smile any of the animals had seen in their entire lives. It was like a small ray of sunshine peeking through thick, dark clouds. They knew the sun was there...they just hadn't seen it in so long.

Mae the Rooster got a tear in her eye as she looked at her friend and said quietly, "I've missed that smile!"

A Twisty Tale

All the animals had the same reaction at first as they started to see their friend come back to them. It didn't take long for Abby to break the sentimental moment, though, by doing a backflip and squealing, "It's working! It's working! She's coming back!"

This was so encouraging to all the animals that they found new excitement after so many months of the same ol' thing.

Days turned into weeks and Michelle's smile was now a permanent fixture around the farm. She even found herself laughing when one of the animals did something silly. That sound was like music to their ears.

One day, Abby was resting in the shade over by the gate having a conversation with Princeton the Horse.

"She looks better every day, don't you think?" Abby said with a contented smile on her face.

"Most definitely!" said Princeton.

They looked at Michelle who was being visited today by one of the Zebra Twins named Rei. Rei was a ball of sunshine who had a presence that just made people feel better. Abby and Princeton noticed something very odd today, so much so that they both stood focused on Michelle while standing intently on all four legs. They didn't know if it was the heat of the sun or if they were imagining things but there seemed to be a wave of heat between Michelle and Rei.

"What is that?!" whispered Abby.

"I don't know!" whispered Princeton.

Mae joined Abby and Princeton when she noticed their eyes deadlocked on Michelle and Rei. Mae knew what they were seeing.

"I've noticed it a few times," she confessed, "and my family has told me about it growing up as a kid. It's energy. We all have it inside of us. Some days we have low energy, some days we have high energy. When we share good energy with people we love, we can usually feel it. It feels like a warm hug or a swelling heart. It makes us smile or tear up with joy. It feels really good when someone sends us love or affection or appreciation. Most of the time we don't get to see it...we only get to feel it. Rei is really good at it though. I think Michelle can feel it. Look at her smiling right now. She's smiling with her whole face. Who knows? Maybe it's helping her in ways that we don't even understand.

Mae, Princeton and Abby just stood and stared in awe. They watched as this wavy energy that looked like a wave of heat moved from Rei to Michelle like a breeze.

Abby tilted her head with a softness in her eyes and said, "I think Rei is sending Michelle a hug."

Mae and Princeton both nodded and whispered in unison, "I think so, too."

Nub's words in the dream of all dreams drifted through Abby's head again. "There are healing powers available to all that are far beyond your imagination."

Abby nodded in agreement. "Yes, there are."

A Twisty Tale

The Sweetest Sound

7.

Over the last several months, the hot days gave way to cool and rainy days. But that didn't stop Michelle from coming out to be with the Animals. It was her favorite place to be by far, and the humans and animals knew it.

Michelle was wheeled to a dry corner in the barn with a blanket on her lap and a roof to keep the rain off her. From this cozy little corner in the barn she could watch Princeton the Horse do his dance routine. Princeton often got to be the star of his own show and he was always willing to perform for Michelle and all the animals. Today was especially beautiful because he had a rainbow as a backdrop after a fresh winter rainstorm.

Abby had made her way onto Michelle's lap, Mae was right by Michelle's side and all the other animals had their noses pressed to the gate watching Princeton's every move. This cozy moment would go down as one of everyone's favorite memories. Michelle smiled and sighed as she watched Princeton perform gracefully. Abby mirrored that sigh as if to agree with Michelle.

"I could watch him all day," Abby whispered.

"Me, too!" echoed Michelle

A Twisty Tale

All of the animals stopped and wondered if what they just heard was real or part of this moment that felt like a dream. They slowly turned to look at Michelle and Princeton joined in the wonder as he made his way to the fence.

Mae gently pressed, "Michelle, did you say something?"

Michelle smiled and nodded and reiterated, "I said me, too."

It was, by far, the sweetest sound they had ever heard. Princeton began to prance, Mae began to crow and Abby began to squeal with delight.

This beautiful, cozy moment in the barn was one they would never forget and these words were the start of many more to come.

Over the weeks, Michelle was able to express herself again and again using words, facial expressions and emotions, and the animals were there for her at every turn. Michelle was now able to emote all the things she was feeling—joy, anger, delight and frustration, and all of her words were there for her. Over time, she had fully gotten her speech back and this made all the animals very happy.

One cool winter day, and for a reason that no one could pinpoint, Michelle just wasn't herself. She struggled with holding things, getting places and was feeling a little blue and very frustrated. Abby noticed this from across the

field and felt the need to let her skills at being a Therapy
Pig shine through.

"Michelle, did I ever tell you about a dream I had when
you were in the hospital?" Abby found herself finding her
storytelling voice.

"No," said Michelle, "But I'd like to hear it."

"One night, I was laying in the hay right over there. I was
feeling really down that night and I was missing you
terribly. You know what I did? I made a wish on a star.
Now, I don't know if I was dreaming or not but what
happened next was magical. A beautiful golden light
came down and landed right in front of my nose. It
looked like a miniature sunball. In my dream, I think it
was my wish coming true. My wish seemed to whisper

words into my mind telling me that you are strong and brave. It whispered that there is an energy in this world for everyone and that it can help us in the most unimaginable ways."

Michelle's eyes were wide as Abby continued with her story.

"This golden orb reminded me that you have the ability to heal your injuries both mentally and physically. It said to remind you of these things when you are tired, angry, frustrated and afraid. It also said to love you and trust the process."

Abby made her way onto Michelle's lap and nuzzled herself into Michelle's arms.

"So, this is me loving you when you are feeling frustrated reminding you to trust the process."

"Abby, you are a wonderful Therapy Pig."

The two snuggled under the stars, feeling all the wonderful feelings of being loved and cared for. Michelle's frustration lifted off her at that moment. She was left with nothing but gratitude.

A Twisty Tale

Moving and Shaking

8.

Over the next several months, winter had made its way to spring and signs of new life were popping up everywhere. There were blossoms on the trees, new chicks hatching in the chicken coop and the sun was like an old friend coming back to say hello.

Over the last several weeks, Mae and the Zebra Twins had been working Michelle overtime with leg lifts and stretches. Mae was in a very familiar role as she pushed Michelle with her exercises.

"Boy, Mae, you sure are bossy." said Michelle as she was complaining about all these leg exercises she had to do.

Mae waddled over to position herself right in front of Michelle to be sure that Michelle heard her message loud and clear.

"Michelle, they said you would never talk again. They said you would never walk again. They said not to get our hopes up. Well, here we are and you are talking up a storm, aren't you? You've already proved them wrong about nearly everything. For goodness sake, you even painted a picture of Abigail Von Phygg. You PAINTED A PICTURE. So, let's not stop now. Michelle, you're writing a new ending to your story. In your story, are you walking?"

All the animals stopped in their tracks to witness this showdown. They knew Mae could be pushy but they hadn't seen this side of her in a while.

Michelle looked at Mae and found a part of herself that she forgot she had. She found her fight.

"Not only am I walking in my story, I'm riding Princeton bareback," Michelle declared.

Princeton neighed in delight and began to prance as if to strengthen his legs, as well.

Mae looked at her with determination and stated in a matter-of-fact way, "Good, then let's get those legs ready."

Over the next several weeks, Mae, the Zebra Twins and Mack worked with Michelle to prepare her for her first steps. They even called in Alister The Lion for reinforcements. They knew they'd need someone very strong for Michelle's maiden voyage on her rediscovered legs.

"Alright," said Mae as all the animals gathered for Michelle to take her first steps. "Are you ready, Michelle?

Alister is right by your side. He'll help give you strength and balance."

All the animals and the humans gathered around as Alister positioned himself by Michelle's side.

"You know," said Alister, "the hardest part is deciding to walk. The walking part is easy. Are you ready?"

Michelle looked at Mae who had one wing up high in the air.

"Queue music!" shouted Mae as she swooshed her wing to the ground signaling rock and roll music to play on all the outdoor speakers around the farm.

At that moment, Michelle's favorite rock song was blasting from the speakers, giving Michelle the extra boost she needed to stand on her feet. All the animals were banging their heads to the beat as if to create a harmonic wave that would help carry Michelle the seven steps from her wheelchair to the gate to pet Princeton.

There wasn't a doubt in anyone's mind that she could do it. Michelle stood, steady on her feet with her favorite song playing. She found a fire inside that moved her right foot one step ahead to be followed by her left foot. Michelle grinned as she found her momentum and as her muscle memory kicked in. Her body remembered how to walk and it took another step to three and then another to four. The animals were fired up and singing and Mae was strutting right by her side. The music was building and so was Michelle's confidence and she took two more steps forward. Michelle looked around at all these faces twisted in rock-n-roll Stank Face and laughed. She realized that they all knew this was an absolute guaranteed outcome. Her friends had no doubt that Michelle would be able to walk again. At this moment, neither did Michelle. She took that final step toward Princeton, put her fingers in the all-too-familiar rock and roll formation and sang along with the chorus.

"Well I'm ba ha ha hack." sang Michelle as the animals joined in, "She's ba ha ha hack!"

They all cheered and danced and crowded around Michelle. It was the most amazing thing this family of animals had ever seen.

Abby nodded in agreement and said quietly to herself, "She's back."

New Habits

9.

Time passed and it was a particularly hot day on the farm as the dead of summer was upon them. It was one of those scorching hot days that sent all the animals running for the nearest shady spot. Mae was relaxing in the corner of the barn somewhere between heat exhaustion and a nap and Abby was on the hunt for some cool mud to roll around in.

Michelle was resting in her wheelchair next to Mae, deciding whether or not to roll herself inside for lunch.

Over the past several months, even though walking had become a much more normal exercise in her life, she used her wheelchair as a resting place in between walks.

Mae, trying not to exert too much energy by talking, lightly whispered to Michelle, "Are you ready for your exercises?"

Michelle said, "No, I think I want to just sit here with my iced tea and snacks in my lap and relax."

Mae cocked her head to the side and said, "But that's all you did yesterday."

Michelle said with a bit of defiance in her voice, "Yep, and that's all I'm going to do today."

Mae, understanding how the heat was making the idea of exercising sound awful, decided to use this moment in a slightly different way. Mae picked herself up, sweated with each step toward Michelle and got her attention.

"Michelle, do you know how all of the great athletes became great? Do you know how all of the great artists became great? Do you know how all of the great musicians became great? Practice. Repetition. It had to become a part of them. Do you know that whatever you do over and over and over you will get really good at? Now, I know it's hot so we can arrange to do your exercises when the sun goes down…but I really think we need to have you do your exercises every day. We can't let skipping exercise become a habit."

"I don't want to."

Michelle was starting to get feisty. Maybe it was the heat or maybe it was all starting to get to Michelle, but today she was stubborn as a mule.

Mae took a deep breath and saw Abby from across the farm. She mouthed, "Remind her!"

Mae remembered the motto all too well. Nub's words came flooding back. "Remind Michelle of who she is when she is tired, angry, frustrated and afraid."

Mae decided a walk down memory lane was in order.

"Michelle, do you remember that time when everyone told you that you couldn't drive a tractor because you were a girl?"

Michelle looked at Mae curiously and said, "Yeah...and I proved them all wrong."

"How?" Mae asked.

Michelle looked off into the horizon as she remembered all the nights she spent practicing on the tractor when no one was looking. She remembered working the gear shifts, learning how to steer this beast of a machine night after night.

"I remember! It took me weeks to get good at it but I finally did."

Mae smiled and said, "Why did you need to drive the tractor so badly?"

Michelle had the best answer to this question. She simply said, "Because I wanted to."

Mae asked Michelle this question already knowing what the answer would be.

"Michelle, do you want to ride Princeton?"

Without hesitation, Michelle answered, "Of course I do!"

Mae smiled and said, "Great. But we have to exercise to get your legs strong enough to do that."

Michelle knew that it was her stubborn nature that she had used her whole life to prove people who bet against her wrong. She realized she was being stubborn in a way that was working against her.

"Ok, Mae. When the sun goes down, let's do our exercises. I don't want to, but I will."

Mae smiled and headed back to her shady spot. She began to wonder if that stubborn streak was nothing more than misguided passion. One thing she knew for sure...don't tell Michelle she can't do something she wants to do.

From that day forward, Michelle never missed a day of exercises. The funny thing was that one day, it stopped being "an exercise" and started just being life.

Progress Makes Cupcakes

10

The farm saw another autumn and winter and life here became pretty predictable. Michelle was getting stronger on her feet, the wheelchair was used only for transport these days and the pace of life was quickening. Tasks that used to take Michelle 15 minutes to do were now happening in less than 5 minutes. All of the animals were pleased and life on the farm was like old times with one small exception: today was Michelle's birthday.

"Hey, Mack!" whispered Mae.

Mack looked at Mae wondering what all the secrecy was. She whispered as well as Mack could whisper, "What's going on, Mae?"

"It's Michelle's birthday today and I want to throw her a party this afternoon. I've already made the cupcakes but I want you to be in charge of the gift. Work with the others and come up with something great. You can do it while we're at the doctor's office."

"I'm on it, Mae."

Mack gave her a wink and called a meeting to order immediately.

Mae tried to camouflage their secret meeting so as not to tip off Michelle.

"Thanks for looking into fixing the well for me, Mack." Mae was sneaky when she needed to be and her wiley ways paid off. Their meeting stayed a secret and Michelle didn't suspect a thing.

Today was Michelle's regularly scheduled doctor's appointment. As the animals watched Michelle and Mae drive away they knew they only had an hour to have their secret meeting and get the gift.

Mack called the meeting to order.

"Everyone, we have a job to do. It's Michelle's birthday today and we have been tasked with a very important job. We need to get Michelle a gift. Any ideas?"

Hunter thought for a moment and piped in with a huge suggestion. "I know! How about a new dress and a new pair of shoes?"

Princess looked at Hunter with a strange look. "When have you ever seen Michelle wear a dress?"

Hunter agreed and went back to the drawing board.

Princess exclaimed, "What about art supplies? She painted that picture of Abby, remember?"

Princess' idea was met with lukewarm enthusiasm, a few "hems" and a lot of "haws."

Then the Zebra Twins popped up with the same answer, almost as if it was rehearsed.

"What about an Amethyst?"

"A-what-a-thist?" said the group?

"An Amethyst. Not only is it Michelle's birthday gemstone, it's purple, it's beautiful and it has wonderful energy."

The group seemed excited. They didn't know if it was the idea of a crystal as a gift or the Twin Zebra's enthusiasm but they were in.

"Ok, gang," declared Mack. "Amashmist it is! Scour the ranch, look under the dirt, ask the neighboring humans. Let's find this Amashmist and meet back here in 30 minutes."

The animals went to the 4 corners of the farm looking for the beautiful Amethyst. They knew it was a crystal, they knew it was purple and they knew they'd find it. It only took 25 minutes for the animals to scour the grounds and they all came back with what they thought was an Amethyst...even if they couldn't pronounce it very well.

"Ok, everyone…" Mack shouted as she called for the group to gather again. Mack looked around the circle and saw that everyone had dug something up, knowing she'd have to rely on the Zebra Twins to correctly identify the stone.

Princess the Rabbit tossed a stone in the center of their circle. It was a black stone and they all huddled around in curiosity. The Zebra Twins inspected it closely.

"As nice a stone as this is, Princess, it is not an Amethyst. That's just a river rock from the creek bed," The Zebra Twins observed.

Groans could be heard from all the animals.

Hunter stepped up with a stone that he wanted the Zebra Twins to inspect. He had discovered a white stone and was pleased to toss it into the circle. The Zebra Twins looked at it, sniffed it and laughed.

"Hunter, did you find this over by the campfire area?"

Hunter nodded and said with confidence, "I sure did."

They chuckled to themselves and said, "This is a marshmallow."

Everyone erupted in laughter, including Hunter who decided to eat his treasure now that it was not going to be wrapped as a gift.

Holly the skunk, who tended to keep to herself, decided she wanted to participate as well. She tossed a brown stone into the circle for inspection.

The Zebra Twins walked over to the stone to give it a look and knew immediately that this was not a stone. They could tell by the smell that it was something not nearly as pleasant as a marshmallow. They didn't want to embarrass Holly so they decided to dig a hole and bury this "treasure" in the ground.

"It's not an Amethyst but it sure does help fertilize the soil so let's bury it so it can do its job, shall we?"

All of a sudden, they heard Princeton neigh with excitement. Princeton had dug a deep hole in the center of the horse ring and found something purple and shiny!

The Zebra Twins looked at each other and simultaneously grinned. They each remembered.

"That's right, we almost forgot! Before there was a horse ring, there was just an open field. When the team came out to prepare the field to build a horse ring, the owner of the property at the time decided to bury three Amethysts deep down in the ground. The owner said it would help keep the riders and the horses in good spirits. Princeton must have found one."

All the animals ran over to the hole and peered inside. What they saw was a beautiful, deep purple crystal. It was gorgeous and it was the perfect gift for Michelle.

"Do you think it's ok to take it from the ground?" asked Princess.

"Why don't you ask it?" said Holly

"Ask it? You mean talk to a rock?" sneered Hunter

One of the Zebra Twins said, "If everything has energy, then that includes water, trees, and, yes, even rocks."

Princess got down in the hole with the Amethyst and pointed her sweet little rabbit nose to one of the purple crystal points.

"Do you mind coming out of the ground and being one of Michelle's friends? She has a lot of friends. We're like family."

Princess lifted her ear and held it very close to the Amethyst waiting to hear an answer. All the animals were silent. Yes, even Hunter.

No words were spoken but at that very moment the sun came from behind one of the clouds and shone right down on the Amethyst. Princess gasped in delight.

"I think that's a yes." said Princess as she clapped her bunny paws with delight. All the animals pitched in to pull this stone out of the ground so they could get it cleaned, polished and ready to give it to Michelle.

Hunter shook his head while still protesting, "I don't believe we are now talking to rocks."

One of the Zebra Twins reminded him, "Hunter, do you remember that story from long ago? A story about a doctor that could talk to the animals. Everyone thought that was crazy at the time. But now look...we can talk to Michelle and Michelle can talk to us." Hunter considered this for a moment and seemed to agree.

"Fine, fine," he said, "But don't expect me to give it a bath."

The animals were just finishing up their polishing of the Amethyst when they heard a car pull up. It was Michelle. She was back from her doctor's appointment right on time. They decided to place the Amethyst on a shelf in the barn out of sight until it was time for her to open the presents.

The animals walked to the car to greet Michelle who was in a particularly good mood.

Mae stood in front of Michelle and announced to the group. "Not only is it Michelle's birthday today but the doctor told Michelle that her progress has been extraordinary. She is surprising everyone, the nurses, the doctors, everyone." All the animals cheered and Michelle smiled from ear to ear.

Mae looked at Mack for confirmation that the gift was ready to go and Mack replied with a confirming wink.

A Twisty Tale

Mack cleared her throat.

"Michelle, if you would kindly follow us to the barn, we have a birthday present we'd like to give you."

Michelle loved presents so she followed the parade of animals into the barn to see what they had in store for her. Abby made her close her eyes for the last 10 steps so as not to spoil the surprise, but she held onto Nicholas for support since this is the first time in a long time that she walked with her eyes closed.

Mae, who never missed any of the important moments, whispered in Michelle's ear, "You can open your eyes."

Michelle's eyes opened as she feasted her eyes on the most beautiful crystal she'd ever seen.

"It's an Amethyst, and it's gorgeous," Michelle said breathlessly.

All the animals stared at Michelle admiring the crystal. They could see how much their gift meant to her and they were all so relieved to see their hard work paid off. They shared the story of how it had lived underground for so long and learned how they all pitched in to make this moment so perfect.

At that moment, Michelle didn't know what she loved more, the crystal or her friends who had put so much into making this birthday so special. Her party continued for several more hours. There were cupcakes and more presents, stories of all the progress Michelle had made while reliving nostalgic moments as a family.

As Michelle blew out her candles, all of her friends knew what she secretly wished for, because they had all wished for the same thing on their birthdays.

It was a great day, and all of the friends gathered around were reminders of how lucky they all were.

A Twisty Tale

Princeton

11

Another spring came and went and life on the farm was as joyful as ever. The animals were all getting on in age as were the humans, but their hearts were bigger than they had ever been. The last few years taught this family what really matters. It taught them the importance of sharing quality time with loved ones, helping people to stand up when they have fallen and laughing as much as possible.

Michelle was contemplating this very thing as she was sitting on a bench with Abby, staring at Princeton who was doing his morning run.

"Abby?" questioned Michelle, her words almost seemed to knock Abby out of a trance. Watching Princeton run could make anyone lose track of time.

"Yes, Michelle?" said Abby, now giving her friend her full attention.

"Why do you think that accident happened? I mean, I know how it happened, but I guess I'm wondering if it was actually a gift after all."

Abby thought about the question for a moment and then asked, like any good therapist would, "What do you think?"

"I think I'm a better person today because of the accident. I think that before the accident, I was running around DOING a lot of stuff. Since the accident, I've been much more present. I care much more deeply for my family and friends. I learned how strong I actually am. I was reminded of the importance of believing in yourself, hard work, and the body's ability to heal itself. I learned that nobody gets to tell me what I'm capable of besides me. I learned to trust my body's ability to heal."

Michelle took a pause and looked up in the sky and then continued.

"I learned that there is something out there, something much bigger than me, and I learned to trust it, even though I may not totally understand it. And I learned that love is important...really, really important, because you just don't know what tomorrow might bring."

Abby smiled the most contented smile.

"Michelle," Abby said, "that moment where everything seemed to break down; that moment that we've been referring to as an accident...doesn't seem like an accident at all now, does it?"

They both smiled and stared at Princeton who seemed to almost be preparing for something.

Michelle stood up and walked to the fenceline. She was strong on her legs and walking was now a normal part of her life. She hadn't used the wheelchair in over a year.

Princeton walked to Michelle for some affection and silent conversation.

"Be gentle with me, girl," Michelle said.

Princeton agreed by nodding his head.

With that agreement, Michelle opened the gate and walked into the arena. This caught the attention of all the farm animals as they headed with purpose to see what was going on. They all remember Michelle being a champion at riding Princeton all those years ago, often without a saddle. Michelle had slowed down since that fateful event in the barn but so had Princeton over the years.

Michelle, using the fence as leverage to climb aboard Princeton, was able to gingerly make her way onto the sway of the majestic horse's back. Once again she found a strength she didn't know she had. Mae, finding herself incredibly nervous about this adventure, decided to trust Michelle's instincts and not interfere. But she didn't take her eyes off Michelle for one second.

All the animals stood back, holding their breath. Some were praying, some were sending energy, some were confident that this would be the ride of Michelle's life. None of them blinked for fear of missing this unforgettable moment.

Michelle was able to situate herself squarely on top of Princeton and her legs and body automatically remembered how to hold on and communicate with this lovely horse.

Princeton started gently moving forward and finding his rhythm and so did Michelle. They had forgotten how beautifully they rode together so long ago. But now, their heartbeats were in perfect sync and the sound Princeton made as he galloped was like a song; a song this farm hadn't heard in a very long time.

The animals looked on, with tears streaming, as Princeton carried Michelle around the arena. Hunter, with his heart full, cried hardest of all. Mack was fixated with joy in her eyes, and the Zebra Twins shook their heads in awe and delight. Princess clapped uncontrollably while Holly and Nicholas stood in amazement.

Mae and Abby knew that this moment, this moment right here, was the moment Michelle had been working toward and they were privileged beyond words to have a front row seat.

Abby whispered to Mae, "Look, on Michelle's right shoulder...do you see it?"

Mae looked carefully as Michelle rounded another gentle corner and she spotted it. A sweet little golden orb.

"Nub!" they both whispered.

Mae said sweetly, "Nub wasn't going to miss this moment for the world."

Abby paused for a moment and said, "I guess we all have a lot more help than we can possibly imagine."

In that moment, with the animals witness to what some would call a miracle, they were all reminded of some beautiful things. And with the music of the gallops ringing out throughout the farm, and the vision of Michelle riding Princeton in full view, they all realized that living a life with love, family, purpose and determination is precious.

Nub's words seem to emanate from this ride and remind every spectator of the message he delivered all those years ago.

"Trust that Michelle is strong and brave. Trust that her mind and body know how to heal and be well. Trust that there are healing powers available to all that are far beyond your imagination. Love and support her. Remind Michelle of these things when she is tired, angry, frustrated and afraid. Share this message with all the animals on the farm. Love her and trust the process."

Everyone breathed a sigh of pure elation and smiled with their whole being.

Today was a magical day and they all asked themselves, "What else is possible?"

A Twisty Tale

Also from
The Zen Room

If you're looking to read more material from The Zen Room or take some online courses, check out these resources below.

Book: "Lessons from The Zen Room"

Online Courses: www.TheZenRoom.net

In-Person Classes: on www.TheZenRoom.net

A Twisty Tale

About The Authors

Dawn

Dawn is an Author, Meditation Coach, Reiki Master Teacher, Certified Hypnotherapist, and Owner of the Zen Room. Using a combination of techniques, Dawn assists her clients who are looking to remove blocks, reduce stress, release energy, seek clarity and experience higher levels of consciousness while tapping into that intuitive part of themselves. Dawn assists her clients in finding untapped potential so they can experience a better life for themselves.

Michelle

Growing up on her ranch in Texas, Michelle participated in different equestrian events at the local rodeo which spawned her desire to become a veterinarian technician. Her passion for animals continued and eventually led her into an equine breeding business. At her core, Michelle was always drawn to helping others. Michelle's compassion to helping those in need led her to become a 9-1-1 dispatcher. Her natural affinity for caring for animals helped her immensely as a First Responder in her community. That incessant desire to help those in need is what led Michelle to co-author this book. It is her hope that her story will inspire those with a long healing journey ahead of them to reach within themselves and walk their path step by step.

www.ingramcontent.com/pod-product-compliance
Lightning Source LLC
Chambersburg PA
CBHW020416130626
46549CB00006B/2582